AuthorHouse™ UK
1663 Liberty Drive
Bloomington, IN 47403 USA
www.authorhouse.co.uk
UK TFN: 0800 0148641 (Toll Free inside the UK)
UK Local: 02036 956322 (+44 20 3695 6322 from outside the UK)

This book is printed on acid-free paper.

ISBN: 978-1-7283-7407-9 (sc)
ISBN: 978-1-7283-7406-2 (e)

Print information available on the last page.

Published by AuthorHouse 09/06/2022

author HOUSE®

The LIFE Treatment

Authors

Olivia Okonkwo MSc

Dr Dean Whittington PhD

1ST Edition

2022

CONTENTS

Acknowledgements

Acknowledgements go to my partner who has supported me throughout my journey of discovering and developing LIFE, someone who provided me with a secure base as I helped to gather the support for this venture. Then there are the university lecturers such as Dr Tine Munk who provided genuine support at university, infusing an inner-city woman with confidence to develop insights around philosophy and practice to eventually move forwards with innovation.

Preface

Being unable to live with your support system as a child can later ricochet across the adolescent and adult life path: surfacing as silent echoes of what may have been - instead of what is. These memory barbs can surface as pangs and stings of wounding memories which pierce an everyday sense of being held in warmth whilst being supported: where the cotton wool of care rapidly dissolves. Meanwhile life spins and unfurls onwards, and the residues require covering up and then hidden. Buried away are the memories - later resurfacing as behaviours to be tamed with discipline and cognitive processing into a machine-like normative state.

In facing the key questions: trauma emerges as a phenomenological or emotional response to the dissolution of security. Routinely within the configurations of the psychopathologies of power, people's experiences become transformed into a thing, something to be measured on a scale of 1-4, inspected and compared within the league tables of abuse.

Hidden are the numerous individual experiences spiralling outwardly as flashbacks exploding in the memory, unexplained illnesses taking over the body: migraines, nausea, and body aches gripping the mind.

In response, what is care? Care provides ontological security. It was through supervision that I came to an understanding around how Criminology and Psychology intertwine, gaining an understanding around how Looked After Children or LAC's as they are labelled are the most at-risk population. Written out of the university discourses however are their plight; absent within Criminology and Psychology are the aftereffects of not being supported in childhood: a glaring scotoma which led me to eventually ponder: Why?

Still the focus is on the physical support of children as their basic needs are met, where the risk assessments becomes over riding and dominant, whilst their emotional well-being becomes secondary due to it less easily being measured. This overriding concern generates the propulsion of the perpetual treadmill where the young person becomes spun around the various treatment services: ensuring their predicament is measured but unfortunately hardly resolved.

In response, this becomes the basis of the formation of a psychologically informed environment: where the foundation of this exploration necessitates the delivery of new forms of relational depth. This leads to embedded scaffolding whilst emitting emotional warmth which nurtures the dreams of the young people within an ideal home. The normal labels attached to a young person denote their non-being (LAC), someone who is 'looked after' but the ideas that underpin the designation require a focus. It is where the concept of 'looked after' entails it is undertaken by someone who is not their original emotional caretaker: often contrasted with its polarity, someone who has endured a rupture and breach of their ontological security.

Any young person placed in local authority care is known as a looked after child; someone who has often undergone a set of bewildering circumstances that has often left them confused. From their perspective they have to make sense of their circumstances whilst having a limited set of experiences upon which to make sense of what is happening to them. Often the young person's sense of bewilderment becomes negated with the need for protecting them from the immediate harm or risk.

A young person becomes designated a looked after child if the parent is physically or emotionally unwell, or if the care needs of the young person require respite care. The young person could be an unaccompanied asylum seeker, with no responsible adult to provide care for them. Alternatively, the child may be at significant risk of harm where the child is subject to a court enforced legal order.

In response a looked after child may end up living with relatives, foster parents, residential children's home, or a residential setting including school or secure unit. A young person can stay in these supportive environments until they are 18 and after this they are provided with transitional support until they are 21. The focus throughout is on enhancing their emotional well-being.

At LIFE young people from different backgrounds and experiences interact and although people have different life journeys the basis of being human are the emotional interconnections that are made. This needs to be undertaken within a safe environment, allowing them to develop their potential.

Statement of Purpose

By working holistically whilst also seeing the potential within everyone the aim is to build towards emotional recovery. This requires drawing on developing positive relationships and generating enhanced life skills, eventually to build towards a personal transformation.

CEO

The *First* Psychologically

Informed Children's Home

A therapeutically based psychologically Informed environment (PIE) (Whittington, 2011) is what LIFE believes is the treatment needed to facilitate emotional recovery amongst young people. After undertaking substantial research combined with personal experience in the care home sector there appeared to be a void in practice used to support young people with their trauma and facilitate recovery. The perpetual cycle of experiencing unhealthy relationships and inconsistent care needs to be re attuned with a new perspective for practice. Psychologically informed practice was originally used amongst homelessness and has not received the recognition that it deserves for the results it produces. Enacting a psychologically informed environment can be challenging as often it is confronted with therapeutic nihilism along

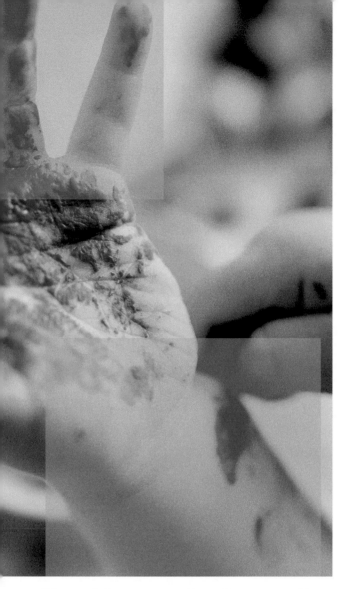

support to attain emotional recovery becomes built in.

The founders of LIFE decided to create the first Psychologically informed children's home for young people aged 10 -17 in 2019. The CEO of life recognised the urgency for a paradigm shift amongst the care sector for young people. There appears to be a consistent experience of reliving trauma and not receiving the treatment and care the young person needs to flourish and engage in the world, to take part in an everyday normalisation.

with resistance, as the therapeutic practice itself is selfless. Therefore, we have used this PIE model as a foundation for our service: all of this being based on supporting numerous individuals to emotionally recover and function outside in previous practice. The focus is on finding a healthy balance of support and autonomy where any additional

It has meant spending a number of years building a team of specialists who have insight and understanding whilst practicing a model of PIE. Working in co-production we have developed a program to develop and support young people in care to build a life ladder out of their current predicament. Our psychologically informed children's home has unique strategies and procedures to enable emotional recovery and to enhance clinical practice. We have developed therapeutic spaces, staff training, activities, groups, and educational classes to ensure that our practice and delivery is safe and meaningful.

We view PIE as a whole instead of it being broken down into bitesize chunks which can be a challenging concept to grasp, we use this approach as this was the original meaning for PIE. It is based on holism as opposed to an overfocus on micro practices to enable recovery. The overall ideal is to generate a paradigm shift which means that all of our work will be Psychologically informed in all aspects.

Understanding LIFE

LIFE (Living Interdependent Focused Environment) provides therapeutic support for young people who have complex needs to rebuild their self-confidence and eventually engage in emotional recovery. An initial focus centres on building trust with young people so they can articulate the various challenges they face and then work with the staff team to overcome them. By understanding that everyone can engage in emotional recovery the therapeutic interventions look at building on the young people's strengths to overcome any challenges that arise, as they seek to enhance their potential. This can only occur by building positive partnerships in the delivery of care.

When reworking the current paradigm, it requires introducing a new set of ideas around building emotional recovery, which entails drawing on the work previously outlined around psychologically informed environments (Whittington, 2011, 2014 2016). By returning to the original ideas, the idea of building a container, thinking about holism, innovation and emotional recovery can be worked through. The aim is to support young people in order to build a sense of the future by reworking the past: where young people may have faced numerous challenges. The aims are to eventually support them to be grounded within the present and eventually develop a sense of the future.

Partnerships and building inter departmental communication are essential in working towards a positive future. This requires drawing upon a person-centred approach, grounded upon embedding emotional literacy to develop a theory of mind. For the practitioner it means viewing the world from a young person's perspective and then building the

support around them so they can grow and excel, by ensuring they can move towards self-actualisation and eventual autonomy. All of this is essential for when they move outside of the care system and enter the mainstream world, where they can still gain support from the service as they learn to cope in this wider environment.

CEO and Founder

OLIVIA OKONKWO

The impetus for the service is grounded upon praxis drawing from both theory and practice to think about how best to support everyone. As someone who is mixed ethnicity and grew up in various environments where I faced several predicaments, I eventually undertook a reflection on my experiences.

I became aware for example that the people around me had assisted me with my emotional growth and from this reflection I began to see how other young people can also be assisted to embark on a similar trajectory: although no two journeys are ever the same. In thinking about how best to support young people I can see that working through early trauma and building a positive sense of the future are essential.

As someone who is involved in setting up the service, my role is in building the container where the staff team can innovate whilst working with the young people to enhance their creativity. It requires working through their defences, needing significant patience in both building, and then sustaining trust. It also entails thinking about the long-term impact of inter-generational trauma, in particular, how this shapes the present-day worlds of individuals: providing the basis to reflect on how to change the young people's internal scripts.

LIFE Vision

At LIFE our vision is to constantly raise the standard of care and leadership for young people.

CEO

Meet the PIE Lead Consultant

DR DEAN WHITTINGTON

Dr Dean Whittington previously worked for 16 years as a psychotherapist within the addictions/ self-medication field, initially based in Deptford SE London, and then latterly working across South London. In the process he devised the first BAME, Women and Men's therapeutic drug services along with support for young people at school.

This therapeutic work unearthed issues relating to trauma in childhood during the 1990's, dynamics that later shaped adolescence and adulthood often hidden from mainstream services. Therapeutic insight became a way of understanding the young people's behaviour as opposed to imposing labels, idealisations and projections upon them. In the therapeutic work undertaken with the homeless from 2006-2011, underlying traumatic issues were unearthed. This discovery provided the basis for the launch of psychologically informed environments, later used by the Dept of Communities and Local Government in a more truncated form. The basis of LIFE is a return to the more expansive holistic and phenomenological foundations of PIE; erased within the current ideations. This expansiveness is highlighted here:

Emotional recovery and positive interventions require building on key individual strengths whilst working towards a life vision. All of this necessitates working through trauma whilst requiring constant reflexivity when entering the bath of steel.

Meet the Clinical Manager

JAY MORALLY

Jay has worked in Health and Social care for over 14 years and started his career working with young people in the probationary system to develop his insight and supervisory skills. Later he worked within well-being services to undertake innovation with adults, drawing upon the tenets of PIE to think about how it could be put into practice. Through praxis he emerged with insight around how emotional recovery is facilitated with people who are cast onto the social margins. The aim focuses upon building choice into their support structure which allows people to develop their autonomy whilst being scaffolded. In establishing this template within his staff team, he fosters the staff's capabilities to generate a holistic psychotherapeutically informed environment.

The Vision

The ultimate aim is to bring about a paradigm shift in how young people

are supported, focussing on working with them to emotionally recover; so,

they can realise their full potential.

The Meaning of LIFE

Living Environment

In supporting a young person there is a recognition that the worlds they formerly inhabited were fractured and therefore to emotionally recovery means overcoming the numerous challenges that have arisen as a result. For the young person it often meant they had to build their internal defences in order to survive within a debilitating environment. Latterly of course, these defences are inhibiting their ability to connect to the wider world. The formation of these internal defences has stopped them from connecting both to themselves, often due to the levels of pain they previously endured: thereby operating as a barrier in connecting with others. Dismantling these barriers is difficult because they previously served a positive purpose but latterly inhibit the young person's growth. Therefore, dissolving them requires considerable patience.

At the same time, when drawing from PIE (psychologically informed environments) it is important to understand that anyone can engage in emotional recovery if they are provided within the appropriate support. What this means is that practitioners have to find the key to enter into a young person's worlds and then work with them to escape their self-imposed citadel by building trust and rapport.

In thinking about developing a psychologically informed environment there are several different facets that need to be reflected upon to generate emotional recovery. Firstly, it requires building a secure base derived from developing trust-based relationships, where each are based on devising individual strategies aiming to dissolve young people's defences so they can enhance their potential. Secondly, it requires empowering young people as the staff team draws on a strengths-based humanistic approach. It also means thinking constantly about building emotional recovery within all interchanges along with thinking about how the wider structure enables this. Thirdly, it requires thinking about how the staff are supported to dissolve the negative impact of the work and in particular the residues of vicarious trauma, such as recognising how this normatively shapes the practitioner. It requires a constant reflection in and upon practice. Fourthly, it requires thinking around how the young people generate social interest and eventually attain a theory of mind by ensuring they are supported in building their recovery capital. Fifthly, it entails thinking about articulating these successes by drawing upon a phenomenological approach when making sense of the dynamics. Sixthly, it requires drawing upon the young people's ideas when thinking about service innovation so that all interventions build bottom up from their understanding, so they are empowered within the recovery process.

The living in environment reflects a young persons need to be valued as this provides a clear signal to them, they are being heard. Fundamentally however, the forms of emotional support which are provided generates emotional recovery. For the staff working within young people in crisis, diffusing the emotional transferences and counter transferences are essential in order to resolve any residues of vicarious trauma. This also requires thinking phenomenologically to dissolve any negative impact upon the self, and this is why reflective practice is essential as it provides the space to innovate and experiment. Ultimately the staff team have to be supported to provide appropriate support to the young people so they can build on their insights and innovations. At the same time, it also entails thinking how the staff team generate emotional recovery within the physical environment. Ultimately by building on the positive aspect of the young person's self-care and enhancing their social confidence, eventually they can actualise themselves within the external world.

It is recognised that young people have the potential skills and strengths to build their self-confidence which then allows them to project their social confidence. This requires them to slowly dissolve their internal defences. Initially these were devised for self-protection as young people created their own security operations to fend off the traumatic void that arose within their childhoods. After a period of time these defences become counterproductive as they halt the person from actualising themselves and connecting to others.

Interdependent

The eventual shift to autonomy is essential for each young person but at the same time there is a recognition that everyone is intertwined within mutual relationships. Furthermore, these can provide the basis for ontological security where a sense of well-being carried within everyday thinking providing a sense of predictability and generating emotional stability. Often people have become self-isolated due to the pain that others have caused; and it requires building trust before they can move into a position of interdependence. All of this requires constant reflection by the practitioners to understand the dynamics which have arisen and how to build social capital.

Focused

The rationale for operating a PIE is that it is an amorphous existential project which allows for an array of ideas to be explored operating without prescription. At the same time, it also entails a focussed intense interaction with each individual in order to ensure they are heard and rendered visible. Another focus is on the individuals' strengths and how these can be supported and enhanced in order to actualise them.

In the therapeutic work there is also a requirement for a focus upon what the young person is revealing about their life history, how they operate within the present along enhancing their dreams of the future. Again, the focus is on how this can be built upon to ensure they attain emotional recovery.

Environment

The wider social and physical environment is crucial in building a young person's sense of self. The young person's ability to self-actualise or transform requires support within their microenvironment, and this is enhanced by building positive partnerships with other agencies within the meso environment. An individual cannot achieve recovery by themselves as it requires extensive support from peers and other practitioners. The aim is to move from the young person's current predicament to attaining a higher sense of self and this requires providing wrap around services so they can generate emotional recovery.

The young person and the practitioner will work together to develop a healthy relationship which will then provide the pathway to recovery.

LIFE Vision

LIFE works with young people of ages 10-17 who have endured adverse life experiences, and this includes thinking about the numerous inter-generational traumas potentially shaping their well-being. The formation of a holistic psychologically informed framework initially provides the support structure or container within which the practitioners innovate to dissolve the impact.

Overall, the LIFE vision becomes enacted by drawing upon a person-centred approach, based on empowerment and the provision of unconditional positive regard, each of which are essential in generating positivity amongst young people. In fostering a secure base, the focus is on grounding the young person so they can build a vision for the future. It also entails working through any previous traumatic blockages, arising within the past so they can build trust within the present. By developing a social network and generating a wider positive connection the focus is on dispelling any therapeutic nihilism: the belief that nothing will change. This can be overcome by building emotional recovery thereby generating a sustainable, positive, affirmative lifeworld. Furthermore, by working with young people who are in the care system, the basis of emotional growth means building on their skills, interests and strengths which becomes the foundation for innovation and developing transferable skills. Ultimately it is about gaining social confidence.

In our young person's home, we believe that developing healthy relationships are the "treatment"

Organisational Structure

The LIFE team are composed of a range of health care professionals who provide a range of different skills based on their expertise, including practical as well as theoretical ideas in developing a psychologically informed environment.

In the provision of care, the focus entails listening to the young person, by acknowledging their moods and still being able to provide support, either alongside, or allowing them distance, so that a trust-based relationship is built alongside the practitioner. It also requires the practitioners building trust with each other to come together as a team who can provide support to each other.

Team Ethos at LIFE:

- A Board of trustees
- Two Service Managers
- PIE Lead Consultant
- A Young Person/Family Psychotherapist
- Children's Social Worker
- Senior Psychologically Informed Practitioner
- Psychologically Informed Practitioner
- Live-in Psychologically Informed practitioner
- Apprentice Psychologically Informed Practitioner
- Resource Psychologically Informed Practitioners
- On Call Pharmaceutical consultancy

Each individual practitioner will attend the following:

- 4 Week LIFE training program
- Reflective practice
- Individual supervision
- Group supervision
- Online and practical training
- 1-1 Support from the Psychotherapist
- 1-1 Support with Social worker
- Individual Support

LIFE Core Values

01 BEING CONGRUENT

When working alongside the young person the therapeutic relationship requires developing a sense of mutuality rather than working within a hierarchy. It means accepting where the young person is at and then working with them to develop their potential. It means each practitioner must work to be on the level when working with the young person, whilst at the same time working with them to be someone higher than who they are in the present.

02 TRUST AND RAPPORT

Trust and rapport building are the basis of any emotional connection and once this is formed it then needs to be nourished. For example, a young person can build further positive relationships with their carers, families, and various agencies. Everything requires a multi-disciplinary approach to develop life ladders to build the individuals potential for emotional recovery. During this time, it is essential that confidentiality is kept whilst these bridges are being built.

03 LIFE PRACTICE

There are number of different forms of therapeutic practice that are undertaken and this flows from the top and then cascades downwards. The basis is in thinking about how the service constantly innovates to meet the needs of the young people. All of this is based on ensuring they develop self-care, a theory of mind to eventually generate social interest: the key components of emotional recovery.

03 LIFE PRACTICE

Practitioners need to be open to change to assisting this transformation as it requires reflecting on what generates success as well as working through the various challenges which inevitably arise. Reflection is based on engaging in continuous learning, and this requires a considerable reflection on how this is overcome. This becomes the basis of the support that is provided.

04 UNCONDITIONAL POSITIVE REGARD

As an organisation we understand and accept that every person is an individual with their bespoke needs. We support a person regardless of their previous experiences, labels, and presentations, placing no further conditions around how they are viewed within the organisation. We also believe that everyone can work towards emotional recovery whatever their previous experiences. This is the basis of the unconditional positive regard that is offered to each young person.

05 PHILOSOPHY OF 'CARE'

As an agency we are involved in constant innovation based on how we deliver care in engaging in best practice. Our aim is to highlight how care provided to the most challenging of young people can be delivered to generate emotional recovery. It means building a 'container' or structure which provides the parameters where the staff can innovate. The aim is to produce a cultural and social paradigm shift to highlight how psychologically informed forms of care promote sustainable change, and from this show that a philosophy of care can be delivered on a larger scale. This can help to transform those most marginalised.

06 INTEGRITY

Integrity means being genuine in what is being delivered requiring firstly viewing the individual as part of a wider world and then working to build their potential. Whilst there is a requirement to be congruent with the young person there is also a requirement to offer integrity. It means holding a professional line when working with young people so that their safety is not compromised. Integrity is therefore combined with ethics.

07 TEAMS OPERATING AS SECURE BASES

In generating a team focussed approach the aim is to offer the young people a secure base grounded upon offering consistent support where emotional recovery is paramount. PIE is infused within the team ethos enabling practitioners to be supported. From this support they can develop positive relationships with young people to develop a theory of mind.

08 EQUALITIES

As a service we work with people from different ethnicities, refugee statuses, social class positions, sexualities, disabilities/labels, and genders meaning that everyone with respect. The focus then is on developing the potential of each young person regardless of their designation by working with their untapped potential not their label.

'LIFE understands the importance of working as a multi-disciplinary team. Part of our approach is to build strong networks and relationships with other local amenities to provide young people with holistic support and care'.

Jay Morally, 2021

The LIFE Model of Intervention

LIFE's Model of Treatment draws on theory and practice and some of these ideas are highlighted below, where the aim is to shift away from seeing people as robots or functioning machines.

When thinking about how theory and practice merge into praxis there are numerous theoretical concepts routinely drawn upon to initiate a PIE. For example, the latter work of Bowlby (1980, 1988) provides a framework for understanding the role of the emotional caretaker. This resonates with Rogers (1951), Adler (1912,1932) Winnicott (1971), Bion (1962), Laing (1959) and Fairbairn (1952) to think both phenomenologically and humanistically. The care home becomes a container which holds the young people where a secure base is built. By working through the young person's defences after understanding that individuals are 'thrown' into fragmented environments which they have no control over, at least initially, that the idea of working towards recovery can be understood. It is through the provision of scaffolding (Bruner, 1974) and working through the schemas of apperception (Adler, 1929) that an individual can develop their life vision (Adler, 1932). The basis is working through psycho-social emotional stages (Erikson, 1952) is to develop a theory of mind and thereby generate social interest (Adler, 1932) along with enhancing a young person's emotional literacy (Steiner, 2003).

Furthermore, by understanding how young people build perceptions of themselves in the formation of the self the practitioner can work with them to ensure their self-esteem is enhanced as previously noted by Stack-Sullivan (1953). For example, they can realise they have choices (Rogers, 1954) and construct an authentic self-image. In building upon these theoretical concepts, the aim is to generate a psychologically informed environment (Whittington, 2016) ensuring that young people build a life ladder out of their current predicament.

Emotional recovery entails working through the numerous psychosocial emotional stages to enhance their growth. LIFE draws also acknowledges the role of the body in shaping the emotions and how the wider world impacts upon individual stress levels.

Overall practioners will be seeking to implement the following:

01 Ensuring the young people understand the importance of healthy relationships with the self and others.

02 Coproducing a Case Formulation.

03 Reflect on how the physical environment along with the social space helps to promote well-being.

04 Adopt a positive psychotherapeutic framework to enhance emotional recovery.

05 Provide evidence through innovation to enhance practice: based upon writing up anonymised confidential case histories and drawing upon phenomenological methodologies to further reflect upon them.

06 Undertake reflective practice throughout to think about overcoming challenges and understanding what works.

07 Understand the long-term impact of psycho-social emotional inter-generational trauma and how this has shaped the young person – by thinking about this in respect of all cultures.

08 Engage in individual and group supervision in order to build the team ethos.

09 Attend ongoing Staff training to introduce new ideas and best practice.

10 Understand praxis: the interplay of psychodynamic/person centred approaches with practice.

Beyond the Label

LIFE supports young people with a variety of needs including behavioural, complex, and emotional well-being/mental health needs. In terms of some of the various labels/diagnoses applied to make sense of these various conditions, we will work with the following:

- Young people diagnosed with mental health conditions
- Gender crisis identities
- Autistic spectrum disorder
- Eating Disorders
- Attention deficit (Hyperactive) disorder (ADHD)
- Well-being Crisis
- Challenging behaviours
- Moderate learning difficulties

- Drug and alcohol use
- Self-harming behaviour
- Gang involvement
- Criminal engagement
- Sex Working
- Attachment disorders
- Offending behaviour
- Complex traumas

Assessment Procedure

Our referral procedure has been devised to make the application process as accessible and efficient for external agencies as possible. Enquires are welcome via phone call, email, and our Q& A page on our website: www.lifetreatment.co.uk.

Outlined referral process:

01 Any queries about the referral process can be made either by phone or by email or on our Q&A page of our website.

02 Once the application form has been submitted via email or on our website, we aim to respond within 3 working days.

03 After reviewing the application, the service manager and psychotherapist will decide how to undertake a further face to face/ virtual assessment of the young person. This will be communicated via email or phone call; you will then be advised to book the assessment through our online booking system on our website.

04 After the assessment has taken place, we will respond with the outcome of the placement within 7 working days.

 * Just to highlight that in some cases, there may be a need for more than one assessment, this is to ensure that the placement is suitable for the young person to emotionally recover*.

We accept referrals from the following services:

- Local Authorities
- Social Workers
- Care co-ordinator's
- Placement managers

- Care giver/guardian
- CAHMS
- Hospitals
- Self-referrals

This assessment provides the young person an opportunity of ask questions and explore how the placement can meet their needs plus allow us to get to know them.

After the initial assessment the LIFE practitioners will contact the young person to see if they are comfortable with attending the LIFE programme. Subsequently a co-produced assessment report along with a risk assessment plus a treatment Intervention plan will be devised. The assessment report will be sent to the young person's placement manager along with the funding authority or social worker to move forward with the next steps.

This will outline the following:

- Funding
- Moving in date
- Tailored treatment plan

- Induction day
- Support Structure provided to scaffold them within the service

'It is the responsibility of the service manager to ensure that the specific criteria and the general principles of the placement are followed'.

Enacting a Psychologically Informed Assessment

Prior to Entering the Sustained Support that is Provided

In the initial assessment the basis of the interaction is taken from thinking about the position of the young person. It also entails drawing upon the tenets of a psychologically informed reflection by thinking about the challenges a young person faces. Then, by drawing on the various facets of good practice the focus is on their strengths and capabilities needed to benchmark how they can grow, develop, and transform into an ideal self. It means working with the young person to co-produce any of the ideations they have. These must be utilised within their growth, so they are central to the process of change. From this form of inductive bottom-up growth of the self the young person can internalise their achievements rather than be instructed and enforced. The assessment is undertaken at the young person's pace and the questions that are asked are based on building their potential rather than being asked just for the sake of filling in the form. The young person will be shown the form and asked to comment on each stage.

The assessment is undertaken face to face or virtually depending on the young person's circumstance. The assessment is in place to ensure that LIFE is able to support the young person throughout their journey: building on emotional recovery, drawing on mutuality and autonomy. Our assessment will be overseen by our PIE consultant and performed by our clinical manager and senior psychologically informed practioner.

Formulation of Needs

All formulations are devised by the psychotherapist in conjunction with the young person as a form of coproduction in working towards their personal goals. This is based on conducting an open dialogue, undertaken by building rapport and trust.

At LIFE our formulations are devised into the following three steps:

01 Developing a formulation

After undertaking an assessment this theory-based conceptualisation is co-produced, operating as a flexible document. It is expected that as the work proceeds the original ideas will change. The overall aim is to work through any defences and blockages that exist in order to develop an integrated self. This can be used to guide any therapeutic intervention.

02 Applying the formulation - Treatment Planning.

The formulation of a general treatment plan for therapy is co-produced, deemed to be flexible as new issues emerge.

A formulation enables the young person to explore the following:

 Their developmental history and ideal self

 Their current position

 Any potential risks

 Ideal well-being/ recovery plan

 Hobbies, Educational, Relationship, Meaningful Work Goals/ aspirations

Formulation will consist of the LIFE team providing a safe therapeutic space for the young person to speak about their past and present experiences. This provides an insight into the bespoke support required to generate emotional recovery.

Safety and Creating a Safe Environment

An important duty of LIFE is to ensure the safety and wellbeing of the young people drawing on a range of clinical and practical tools.

The tools we use to manage risk:

PRE-ASSESSMENT	COMMUNITY MEETING
RISK ASSESSMENT	INCIDENT REPORTS
RECOVERY PLAN	DATA ANALYSIS
WHISTLE BLOWING	PSYCHOTHERAPY
LIFE PLAN	SECURITY AND SELF ACTUALISATION SUPPORT (SASAS)
THERAPY PLAN	
KEEP SAFE PLAN/ FORWARD DIRECTIVE	LIFE SKILLS CLASS
	TALKING
MOVE ON PLAN	PEER MEDIATION
SAFEGUARDING	OPEN SPACE
REFLECTIVE MEETINGS	INTERVENTION FROM EXTERNAL SERVICES AND TEAMS
EXTERNAL MEETINGS	

SUPPORT FROM EXTERNAL SERVICES AND TEAMS

Client information and GDPR

Client information and data protection are regulated under the general data protection regulation (GDPR) to ensure privacy and confidentiality are always maintained.

LIFE complies with keeping clients and employees' information safe.

Communication with External Services and Agencies

Communication and transparency are key components within any relationship and LIFE is focussed on communicating effectively with external services and agencies to ensure the safety of the young people. The needs of the young person and how they are being actualised entails working with external agencies.

Psychologically Informed Actualisation (PIA)

01 LIFE VISION

In working towards their personal vision, young people are encouraged to think and reflect on what practical support they need. PIA draws upon therapy to support young people with their psychological recovery, along with their development, and growth. A family/ young person psychotherapist provides therapeutic support this can be individual, group or even informal pre therapy.

Therapeutic support allows the young person to articulate what exists behind their 'front', something which is normally hidden. The focus is on working with them to shift from their current predicament to a more life affirming perspective.

In order to visualise the forms of therapy available, the following provides an insight:

02 PRE-THERAPY

The pre-therapeutic engagement draws from the work previously undertaken in building psychologically informed environments (Whittington, 2016) and this is essential for establishing rapport and dissolving defences. The next step is to build trust, the basis of a therapeutic relationship which allows the young person to reflect upon themselves. By engaging in pre-therapy, the eventual aim is to engage in therapy for an hour individually at least once a week and these concepts were outlined by Prouty (1997) Sommerbeck (2006) and Whittington (2016).

03 WEEKLY THERAPY

Eventually there will be a shift from pre-therapy to engaging in 1-1 therapy which becomes the basis for long-term recovery. How this occurs is down to the skill of the team in providing a safe environment for the young person to engage with the support that is provided. The therapeutic support aims to draw upon Adler (1932), Rogers (1954), Maslow (1938) Laing (1959) as well as other humanistic/existential theorists within an integrative approach to offer an inclusive environment. This forms by providing a safe and secure space where the individual becomes empowered; and from this they grow emotionally: benchmarked by the individual and the star outcome chart.

04 YOUNG PERSON/ FAMILY THERAPY

We offer the young person/ family therapy to support the young person and their family to find ways to work through their various challenges. In family therapy the therapist works with the families and those in close relationships who are experiencing difficulties with their past and present. The therapist explores their views around their positive and negative relationships to understand the various strengths and difficulties in seeking to think about how to develop a positive framework.

05 LIFE PEER MEDITATION

Conflict can sometimes occur, and this requires resolution and so peer mediation is available within a safe confidential setting, which can be used to resolve conflict with the assistance of our trained practitioners. Peer mediation creates a space for people to make sense of their behavioural and psychological differences to build social interest. Peer mediation also offers space for reflection upon one's own behaviour and provides a space to explore and work upon identified aspects of the self.

"…. Trauma is a shattering of innocence. Trauma creates a loss of faith where there is no more safety, predictability, or meaning in the world along with no safe place in which to retreat. It involves utter disillusionment, because traumatic events are unable to be processed by the mind and body as other experiences are, due to their overwhelming and shocking nature: so they are not integrated or digested. The trauma then takes on a life of its own and, through it continued effects, haunts the survivor, and prevents normal life from continuing; until the person gets help".
(Whittington 2016, Psychologically informed Environments:
Therapeutic Regeneration).

Building a Support Structure

The support structure is devised from the initial secure base that has been formed within the home incorporating the other partnership agencies coupled with the family of origin to build a framework for the young person. This rests upon everyone having similar outlooks and aims, focussing on developing the young person's well-being and building on their strengths at all times.

In working towards their actualisation, a person-centred approach (Rogers, 1954) is essential to ensure a young person is treated with dignity.

Incorporated within this approach are the following concepts:

01 The practitioner is congruent with the young person.

02 The practitioner provides unconditional positive regard.

03 The practitioner shows an empathetic understanding towards the young person.

04 The practitioner is genuine

05 The practitioner undertakes reflective practice to work through any challenges that arise.

By working through these concepts, the aim is to develop self-actualisation - where a person can draw upon his or her full potential to gain a positive sense of self.

STAGES OF PSYCHO-SOCIAL EMOTIONAL GROWTH

Erikson (1950) notes how various changes occur in the development of the self during early years, adolescence, and early adulthood. Normally the young person is supported within their family environment to overcome these challenges as they build trust, gain autonomy, develop their initiative, engage in industry, find their role, and then move towards engaging in intimacy. Normally young people develop a number of competencies which they later draw upon as forms of resilience to enhance their confidence and self-esteem. In drawing on a strengths-based programme many of the young people will need support to overcome significant hurdles as they build their internal capacity to overcome these challenges and move towards self-actualisation.

HOLISTIC TEAM AP-PROACH

The treatment program is overseen by clinically trained health practitioners who enact the PIE model to facilitate the young person's growth and emotional recovery. The everyday interactions are key to generating recovery, but this takes place within an infrastructure. It requires everyone to be part of the PIE, and this entails building awareness amongst other professionals around the aims and objectives of the project. Holism also aspects entail looking at their physical, educational, spiritual and health related needs. It also means working with the young person to connect to the positive aspect of their family to build the secure base to generate a positive sense of self and security.

PRE-THERAPY

As Sommerbeck (2006) outlined traditionally many individuals have been labelled as being beyond therapeutic reach, unable to access traditional forms of therapy due to an inability to sustain their interest. In effect there have been demands for the individual to be 'well' before they attend therapy.

Pre-therapy works with the individual where they are at, and not where a practitioner thinks they should be. These ideas come from Prouty (1997) which are also an extension of Rogers (1951) ideas around how to engage those individuals who normally avoid formal therapy. Many individuals are pre-expressive, young people who have also have often lost their social confidence entailing they lack any ability to engage with a therapist. Pre-therapy aims to work with young people where they are at, and it requires reflecting on the immediate surroundings and how these shape a sense of self. By engaging in grounding with the young person, the aim is to bring their attention into the present. This means finding a common point of contact to generate a discussion with the aim of facilitating the grounding which entails gradually enticing the individual into the here and now. It requires considerable patience and skill to undertake this, and perhaps is one of the most challenging aspects of the work. It also requires considerable being able to recognise the requirement to do this intuitively, becoming a key requirement of the therapeutic work.

This type of therapeutic encounter sets aside the labels placed on the young person in order to build a connection upon which the ability to talk about the self can later take place. Therapy is therefore seen as an ongoing process rather than bounded by a specific space and designated number of sessions. This relates to the experiences of the YP and how they view the concept of 'therapy' which must be expansive including art and play therapy when aiming to engage the young person. In this way the ability to work through various puzzles becomes expansive rather than being based upon verbal communication alone.

INDIVIDUAL PSYCHO-DYNAMIC APPROACH (ADLER 1932/1999)

Prior to Rogers (1954), Adler (1932) the forgotten man of psychotherapy outlined that most thinking is subconscious which then drives human behaviour in a form of autopilot. This is where the individual builds their basic concepts entitled 'schemas of apperception'. These building blocks often dictates the individual's private logic, such as what they think of themselves along with others which then shapes the personal lifestyle: namely, how they interact with others. Simultaneously it shapes their future vision and how they view the future.

One challenge is how an individual's traumatic background shapes these schemas where the secure base becomes fragmented. To initiate recovery requires piecing the self together, work that is often painstaking. Through building the secure base however, the young person can develop a foundation allowing them to they build on this for the future.

PRAXIS

All forms of therapeutic intervention are based upon praxis, the use of theory and action to enhance the development of the self. It requires formulating independent living skills, whilst also creating and sustaining relationships by developing a positive self-identity. Ultimately it creates a space for self-realisation.

Erikson (1950) outlines that finding a self-identity becomes paramount for anchoring the self and thereby generating emotional well-being. This provides a sense of resilience for adulthood and enhances the young person's self-esteem so they can actualise themselves after developing an initial foundation.

"The model, approaches and theoretical thinking is used to recreate a surrogate care giver's role. Through the outlined practice we can provide young people with the care they need in order to experience safety, love, direction, nurture, support, and guidance."
(Olivia Okonkwo, 2020)

Working With Families

In building ontological security as highlighted by Laing (1960) one of the key aspects is being able to build upon positive care and overcome any negativity. Instead, the focus is on building recovery capital with the support of the child and family therapist along with the other practitioners with the aim of developing a secure base. This is a platform which will help the young person develop a wider support network, so they are able to enhance their emotional well-being.

Modes of Engagement

The modes of engagement are explored in the space entitled " LIFE Hack". A LIFE hack in educational space once a week and has been compiled in order to support young people in their development based on the following:

- Relationships and attachment styles.

- The positive benefits of therapy.

- Having a sense of Identity and the role of self-care and self-love.

- Working to emotionally recover.

- Developing goals and aspirations.

- Envisioning the future.

- Financial understanding.

- The role of education in school, college, training provision and apprenticeships.

- Ability to live interdependently outside of the care system.

- Becoming an asset to the community.

- Self-Actualisation.

- Psychosocial stages and how to work through them.

LIFE Hack is a safe space which aims to educate young people both psychologically and practically preparing them for life outside of the service. The Life Skills class has been designed to nurture young people to have the knowledge and understanding to build mutuality and autonomy in order to prepare for their future life experiences. This space creates reflection and guidance by stimulating the interest of the young person to enhance their future ideals, creating an exciting and hopeful path.

The life skills class is conducted once a week by our LIFE skills coach who will be making education feel fun and enjoyable through the following:

- Drama

- Group activities

- Role play

- Art

- Music

- Reading

- Dancing

- Workshops

We have devised this educational space into three terms which is focused on both psychological and practical education and then bringing them together for further development:

Term 1 – Psychological Education

Term 2- Practical Education

Term 3- The combination of both Psychological and Practical Education

Please note: Each term is broken down into 14 lessons , therefore the young people will engage in 42 lessons across the year with an allocated time of 1 hour per session.

Core Structure

The core structure is based on establishing a framework:

BREAKFAST CLUB:

Every morning at 7:00 am all young people will be provided with a healthy nutritious breakfast catering for all dietary/cultural needs. In having breakfast, everyone is provided space and support to prepare for the day ahead. This is undertaken in the provision of a positive atmosphere aiming to build self-confidence.

WEEKLY COMMUNITY MEETING:

The purpose of each community meeting is to build democratic accountability drawing upon the concepts first outlined by John Dewey (1913) by allowing a cross section of viewpoints to be brought to the surface. Any difficulties can then be worked through, and this is not an 'encounter group' as the focus is on building harmony and connection. By developing communication skills and an understanding of the self in relation to others, key skills around actualising the self and deepening personal knowledge for both the individual and the wider group eventually forms due to the levels of interaction that everyone is engaged in. The Community meeting will be held once a week in a communal space and aims to last 40 minutes and will cover the following agenda: (which will be co-produced but based upon the following ideas).

- Check in
- Joining and leaving
- Maintenance
- Suggestions and ideas
- Community discussion
- Queries
- Review of meeting
- Check out

OPEN SPACE:

Open space is a space allocated to the community (young person and practitioners) which allows people to speak about difficulties, dynamics, and relationships: all facilitated by the therapist.

ACTIVITIES DAY:

Activity days take place over the weekend, allowing the young people an opportunity to choose a leisure activity of their choice. The activity day is to enable fun, creating bonding and mutuality in order to provide an alternative to working on the self and enhancing education capabilities. The focus is on undertaking different and stimulating activities.

SUNDAY COOKING CLASS:

The Sunday cooking class is a part of a group dynamic based upon developing practical skills around hygiene, co-operation, budgeting, nutrition, self-actualisation and learning about different cultures, customs, flavours, and food tastes. Cooking falls into the important category of generating autonomy and building life skills. Cooking lessons are part of the learning program as they prepare the young people to gain an insight into health and wellness as they learn to think critically about food production whilst also reflecting on how they consume food and its impact upon the self.

Once a week the young people will be encouraged to decide on a dish they would like to learn and cook as a communal enterprise. Cooking lessons are conducted by a trained chef who will be supporting the young people to work through the various dynamics that arise.

Developing Relationships

Every young person will be provided with a Life Guardian where the focus is on building supportive ongoing relationships with the aim of ensuring that they are sustainable as they work through any practical difficulties. In building a sense of attachment there is room for fun whilst also engaging in emotional grounding (being in the present) and developing rapport. One example is playing a board or computer game that requires co-operation and team building or helping someone take part in a hobby. Other aspects are being with someone as they attend a doctor's appointment or picking people up from school and attending school appointments.

Our LIFE Guardians are supervised by the Service Manager with further input from the psychotherapist and children's social worker. Whilst also working with the young people these LIFE Guardians also maintain contact with external services.

The Responsibility of the LIFE Guardian is:

- To formulate/ establish a healthy attachment and build relationships.

- To work with external services and agencies if required.

- To engage in fun tasks and use this to create a healthy relationship.

- To have at least 1 set session each week.

- In the interactions to critically reflect by drawing on Socratic questioning around perspectives, choices, and decisions especially any that invoke therapeutic nihilism or are self-negatory.

- To provide positive modelling.

- Create healthy relationships.

- Provide a space for reflection.

- Exploring topics of discussion.

- Establish boundaries for the relationship.

- Supporting the young person with goals and aspirations.

These sessions can also be time bounded, discussion led, goal orientated, and outcome monitored if the young person requires this. These sessions can take place on and off site so long as the session provides the client a safe space and usually last an hour but can be extended if needed.

Learning and Education

WORKING WITH EDUCATIONAL AND TRAINING PROVIDERS:

LIFE operates under the aegis of all the various legal statutes in the welfare of the young people. This legal structure provides a secure base, which is drawn upon to develop the potential of the young people in the promotion and encouragement of their educational achievements along with their life goals. All of this is incorporated in the organisational ethos to build a holistic approach.

In understanding the role of the wider ecological environment, the young person inhabits the support provided to ensure they attend:

- Secondary school
- Alternative educational providers (Pupil referrals)
- College
- Home schooling

- Virtual schooling
- Training
- Place of work

We work with all external services such as:

- Schools
- Colleges
- Training providers
- Tutors
- Employers

How do we support education within our service?

We have allocated time twice a week called "tutorial" for young people to obtain educational support with:

- Homework
- Reading
- Applications
- CV creating

- Projects
- Assessments
- Exams
- Coursework

What happens if educational support is ruptured for some reason?

Formal education and training can be a challenge for several reasons potentially shaping the young person's ability to attend formal or informal educational sessions. The practitioners will be seeking to make sense of the various dynamics that arise which entails working with the young person and their educational providers to overcome any difficulties. The focus is on the life vision of the young person and how this can be achieved so their needs can be met.

We offer the following opportunities to support young people whilst they are:

- Appealing against exclusion
- Attending a Pupil referral unit

- Engaged in Home schooling
- Attending Independent training providers

A Support Structure is Provided around the following

- Prompting and preparing young people to attend education
- Parent's evenings
- Events at school
- School trips
- Sports days
- Acknowledgement days (red nose day, world book day, mental health awareness week)
- School drop offs and pick-ups
- Training/ College drop offs and pick-ups

- Meetings
- Open days for college/ university
- Appointments
- Reviews
- Assessments
- Extra curriculum activities
- Detentions
- Isolation
- Exclusion

Education, training, hobbies, and meaningful work are vital for providing a sense of purpose for each individual whilst also maintaining a sense of self both practically and psychologically. In meeting their life vision, the focus is on scaffolding the young person to access support to build towards their ideal sense of self in the promotion of developing a higher sense of self.

TUTORIAL:

Actualising Positive Educational Experiences by working towards specialist training and then moving towards meaningful work are all actively promoted and supported. We provide young people with tutorial sessions so they can complete homework, develop research strategies, and become actively supported so they can ask questions by developing their critical faculties. By working practically, the pre-therapeutic strategies which drew upon building rapport and trust along with being attuned ensure that a psychologically informed environment is built.

A tutorial is also scheduled into a weekly rota and deemed part of the core structure which provides further time to work through any challenges that have arisen. It works on the concept of developing a zone of proximal development (ZPD) where the potential of the person is outlined, and the support then provided to actualise this potential.

LIFE HACK (LIFE SKILLS CLASS)

LIFE Hack provides an opportunity for young people to develop their knowledge of the psycho-social emotional stages and work out how to navigate them.

Meanwhile, the LIFE Hack is where young people are provided with practical support such as learning about finance, budgeting, the role of personal hygiene, nutrition, and health. Apart from gaining financial skills they can also gain active citizenship insights such as the role of bureaucratic systems plus how to write letters of support and engage in challenging decision making within enhanced citizen classes. This

means knowing how to access councillors, MPs' and understanding the various systems that exist, plus how to approach people and understand how systems work. Young people will provide with the soft and hard skills to manage and navigate through everyday life by having the knowledge and understanding how these various systems operate, along with developing their interpersonal skills.

HOW DO WE ASSESS THE YOUNG PERSON'S PROGRESS?

The assessment is ongoing and undertaken every six months drawing upon an informal life skill test (verbal or written pending young person's ability) which enables young people to benchmark their progress.

For further detail on the LIFE Hack Class, youcan request the LIFE Skills Handbook.

LIFE Hack Graduation

Alongside the LIFE Hack class, a graduation will take place once a year after the academic year has been completed. The graduation is a ceremony which provides an opportunity to celebrate success and build self-worth. By being affirmed, a young person is eventually brought into the world where their sense of being is eventually anchored to develop their ontological security. This ensures that they can receive a diploma in LIFE Skills which will be celebrated with the wider community, friends, and family.

LIFE provides two main added value opportunities for the development and growth of the young people:

Obtaining a Driving licence:

We support young people to apply for their provisional licence at the age of 16 and then scaffold young people so they can start their driving lessons from the age of 17. In having the ability to obtain a driving licence, the young person is potentially provided with independence whilst also learning to be responsible in the eventual transition from the care environment.

LIFE Hobbies

LIFE believes that hobbies are necessary in the development of building ontological security, meaning and social skills. LIFE will support young people to develop their potential for example in the following fields:

- ✓ Music/Art/Poetry/Reading/Writing
- ✓ Sport/Physical Exercise
- ✓ Dance/Drama
- ✓ Art/Photography
- ✓ Chess to Bingo

Feedback Procedure

Psychologically Informed feedback is essential for emotional growth. This can either be seen as positive feedback based on affirming the individual or it can be viewed negatively in pointing out any gaps. It is important that of each of these are addressed when building a PIE.

If any young person, local authority, caregiver, or external service wishes to post negative feedback then the following steps can be followed:

01 Discuss the presenting issue with the person first and foremost to see if there is a reason for them to rethink how they are currently interacting.

02 If this cannot be resolved, they can put their feedback within the suggestion box or send via an email to: queries@lifetreatment.co.uk.

03 If it something which requires immediate attention, then the mediation policy will be enacted and if it cannot be resolved an independent support service will be contacted.

04 If the type of feedback requires an in-depth reflection, then the organization will need to bring it to reflective practice. In terms of reporting, it can be done anonymously or by putting a name to the stated concerns. Any learning experience will be communicated to the person who has posted the feedback, so they understand how any issues have been resolved.

Mission statement

Our mission is to deliver emotional recovery and enhanced well-being to ensure young people can build a life ladder from their current situation and enter a world of positivity.

CEO